How to Paint A Rose In Watercolor

by Debbie Waldorf Johnson

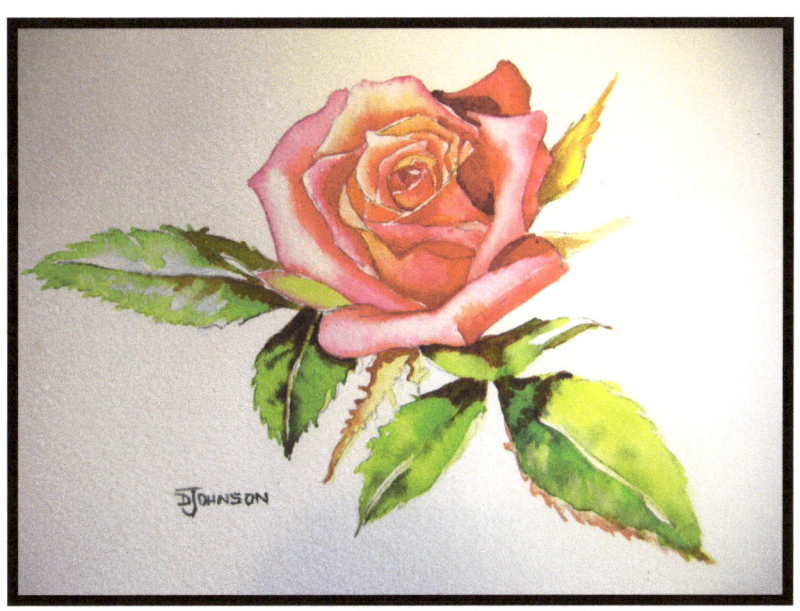

Copyright © 2014 by Debbie Waldorf Johnson

Table of Contents

Review of Basic Painting Skills

Before working on a painting, review some of the basic skills required in watercolor painting.

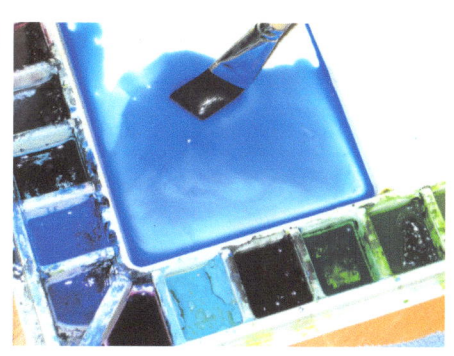

When preparing for a wash (application of paint in a watercolor painting) always begin with a big puddle of wet paint in your palette.

Draw four loose rectangles on a piece of watercolor paper. Each rectangle should be about four by five inches, approximately. Draw these loosely; there is no need to use a ruler!

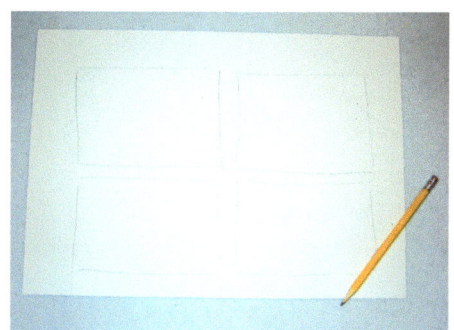

Flat Wash - An even distribution of color in a small or large area. This is the foundational wash for all other washes used in watercolor painting.

Hold your paper in your non-painting hand at a slight angle, about 25 - 35 degrees. Start at the high end so that your paint will float toward the next stroke. Using a 1" flat wash brush, draw a wet line of paint from one edge of the rectangle to another. The paint should be wet enough to leave a bead or puddle of wet paint along the edge of your mark.

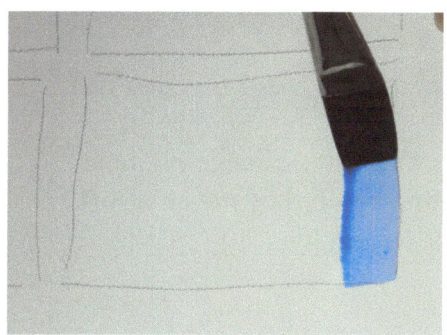

As you pull the next stroke, again with very wet paint, be sure it touches the puddle or bead of paint from the previous stroke. This pulls the wetness into the next stroke. Continue holding the paper at a slight angle to keep the bead at the same edge of the stroke so that you can touch it again when making the next stroke.

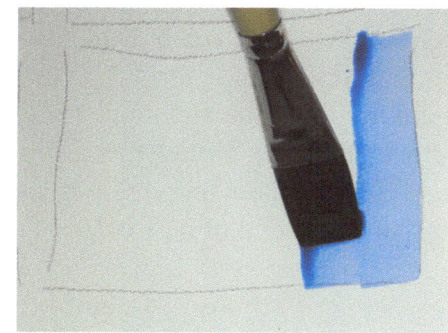

When you completely fill the rectangle, tamp your brush on a paper towel (I use an old wash cloth) and use the relatively dried brush to syphon the last bead of paint away from the wash. Now it is safe to lay the paper flat again. Allow to dry or dry with a hair dryer.

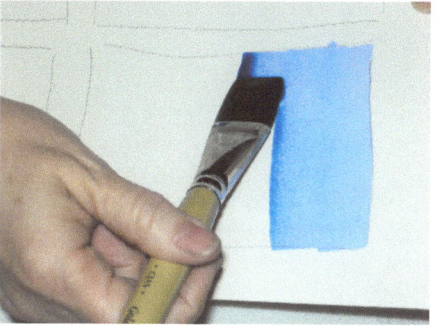

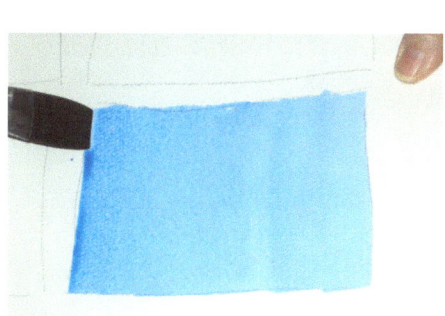

The goal of a flat wash is to create a flat, smooth area of even color.

View a video of this technique at:
http://www.youtube.com/watercolorworks

Graded Wash - A wash that starts with a darker value and progresses to a lighter value.
The same principle that is used for a flat wash is also used in creating a graded wash. The difference is that as each stroke is applied, a small amount of water is added to the palette to make the pigment more diluted. This creates a nice value change, which can be used in almost every painting. It is especially great for skies.

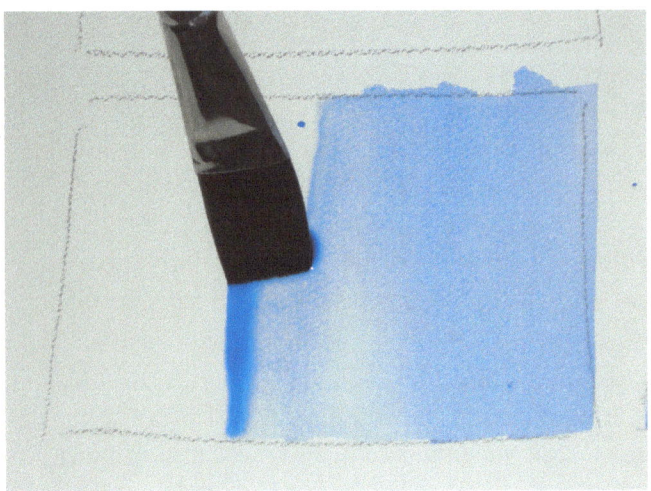 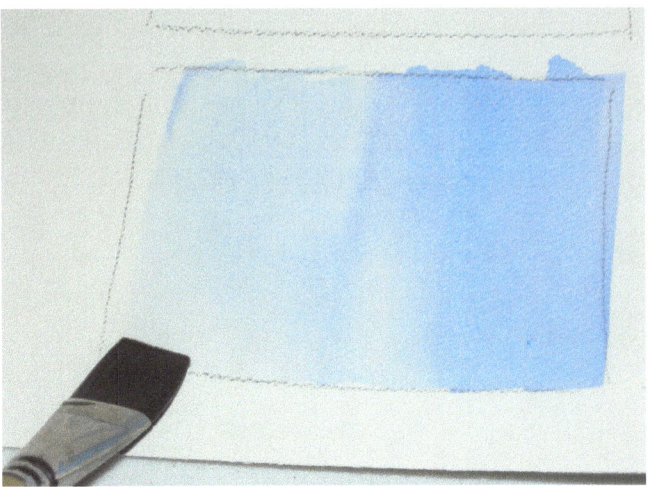

Blended Wash - A wash that contains two or more colors that meet at wet edges to blend together and appear soft.
Again use the same technique to lay down color as you would a flat wash. This time, change pigment part way through. Notice that as the second color touches the bead of the first color, they create a soft edge. If both colors are very wet and the paper is tipped back and forth, they will physically mix to create a soft blend of new color.

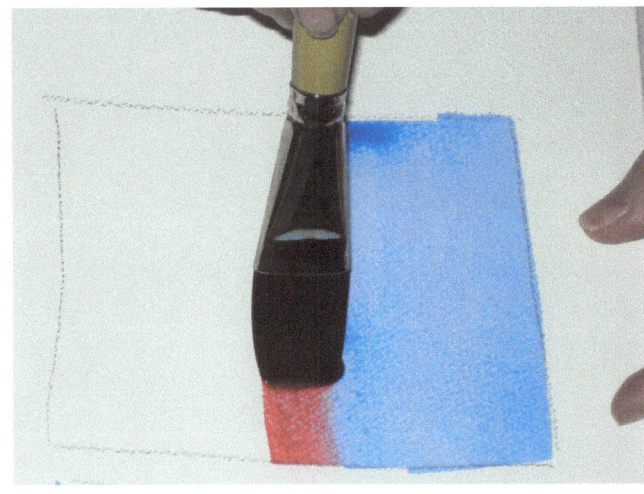 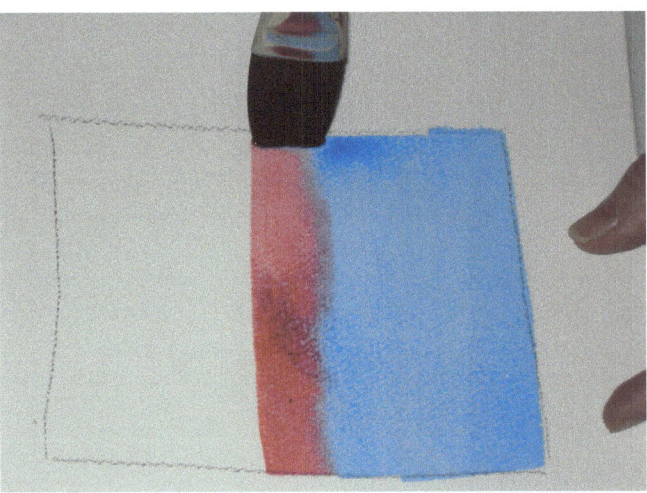

View a video of this technique at:
http://www.youtube.com/watercolorworks

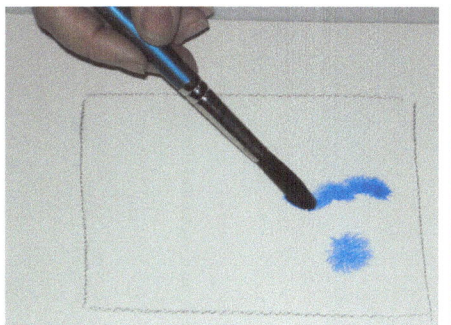 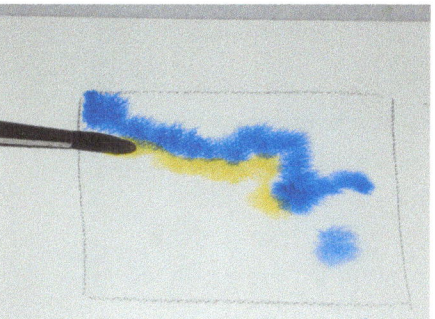 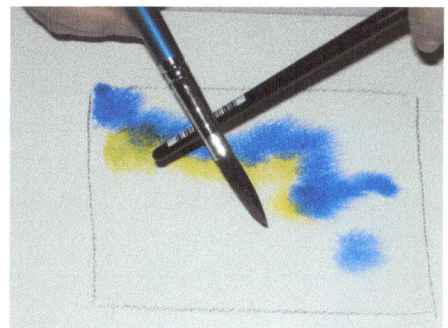

Wet-in-Wet Wash - A varied wash of several colors applied on a wet surface.

Wet-in-wet washes are fun, yet difficult to control. Wet one of your rectangles with plain water or a light color. Completely cover the rectangle. Allow the water to absorb into the paper so there are no standing puddles, but so that there is a glossy appearance to it. Next, drip or paint strong pigments into the wet areas. Use several colors and experiment. You can also tap a loaded brush onto the handle of another brush to splash pigment into the wetted area. Tipping the paper will blend the colors more, leaving the paper flat will help to contol the blending.

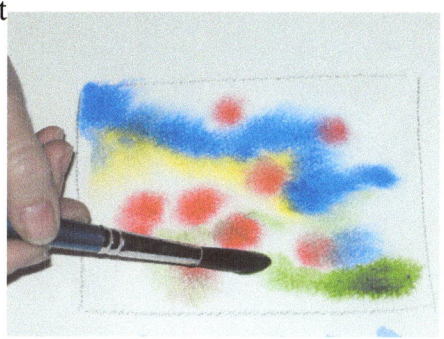

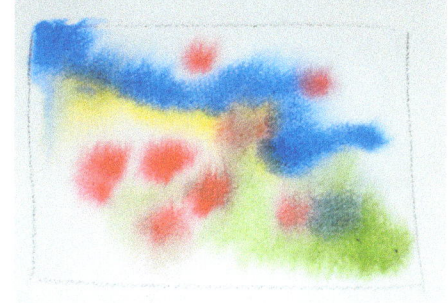

Calligraphic Linework - Linework of pigment developed using all edges of a brush at various angles.

Practice using all of your brushes and see how many marks you can make with each. Hold the brush straight up and down, hold it at a drastic angle, and push and lift it as you pull pigment across the paper. Try to write your name in cursive with each brush you have. Explore what your brushes can do for you!

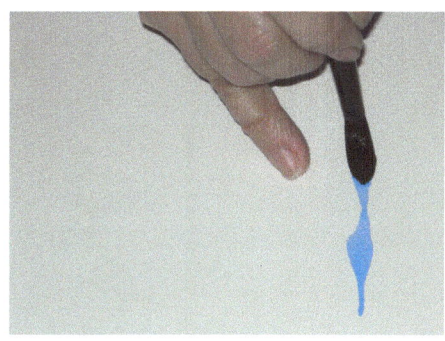 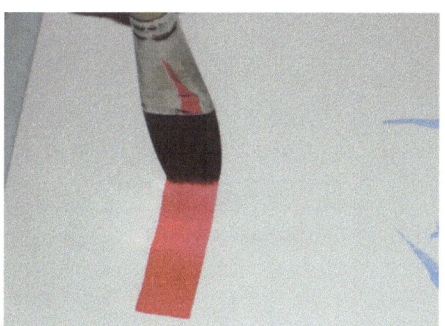 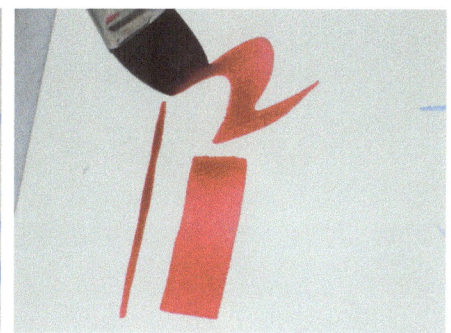

Dry Brush/Scumble - Linework of pigment developed using relatively dry paint and a variety of brush strokes.

View a video of this technique at:
http://www.youtube.com/watercolorworks

Painting References

Always use your own photos!!! Collecting and organizing photos is fun and provides rich resources for inspiration for your paintings. I enjoy looking at professional photographs as inspiration for set ups, but I always use my own objects and photos. Once you find photos that suit your desires for a painting it is time to move on to the next step. I have provided reference photos and a final drawing at the back of this book

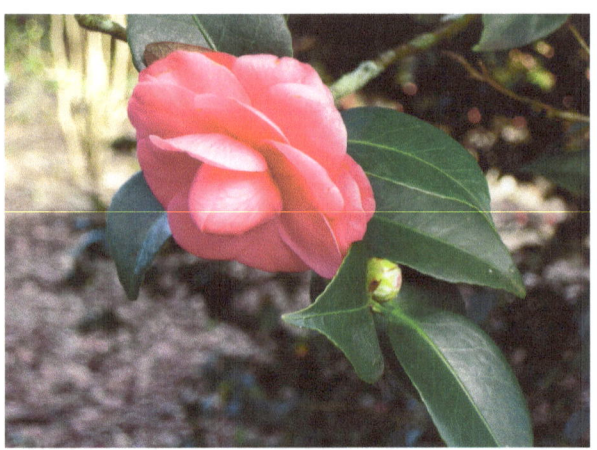

for the project shown in this workbook.

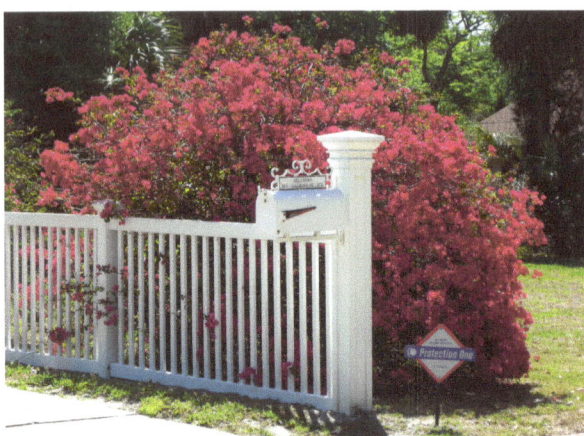

Many artists enjoy painting from life either outdoors, plein air painting, or from a still life set up under controlled lighting situations. I

enjoy plein air, but I also like to work from my photographs because I have much greater control over the lighting and I can work at a slower pace.

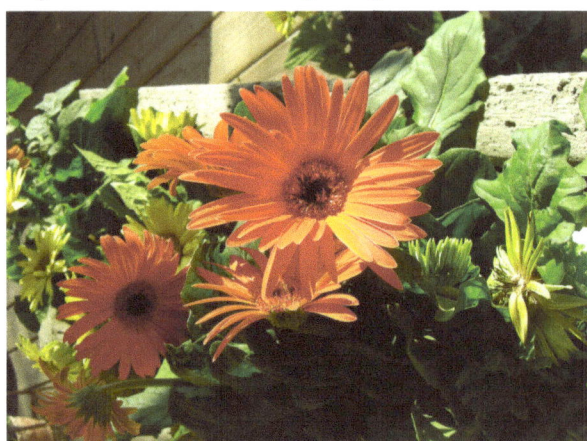

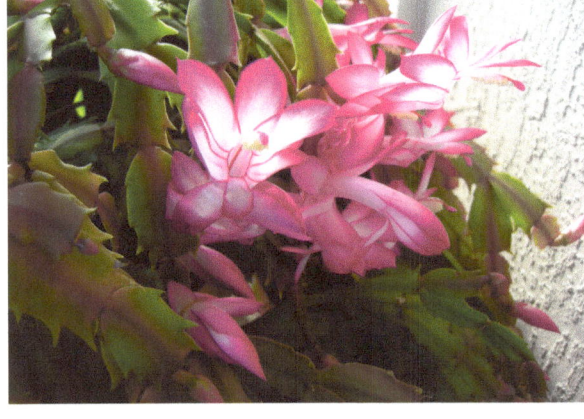

Either way, be sure to use your own resources. Never copy another persons work without their written permission.

Take your time composing your photographs. Be sure you have nice lights and shadows to add depth to your final painting. Look for pleasing compositions and take a lot of photos of each object from many views and angles. Be sure

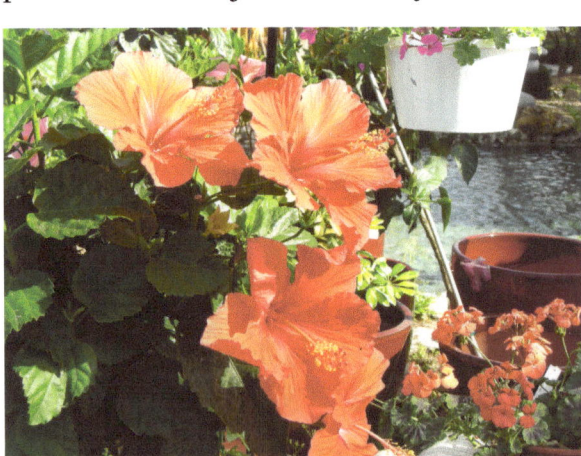

to get some close up shots if you want to remember the details when you get back to your studio.

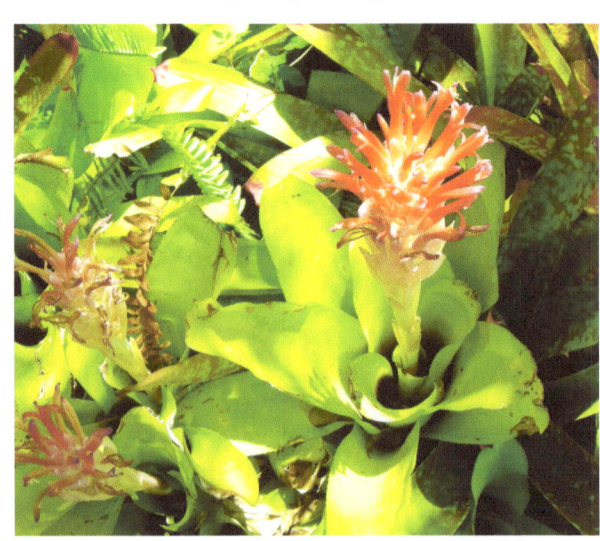

Planning Your Composition

Even though you did a lot of work on your composition at the set-up stage, there is still a little more work to do. The more thoroughly you work out the details beforehand the more fun your painting process will become. Whatever problems you neglect to work out at this stage will haunt you throughout the painting.

All objects can be reduced to the most basic shapes: circle, square, and triangle. From those basic shapes we can add shading and distortion to make cones, rectangles, cylinders, ovals, etc. These simple shapes are found everywhere.

Try to sketch the most basic shapes (triangles, cones, squares, ovals, etc.) from your composition in your sketchbook. Place the objects in a pleasing way on your paper. Don't worry about any details until the basic shapes are in the correct place.

Now you will develop some thumbnail sketches from your basic shapes. Thumbnail sketches should be small and should be used for problem solving before you ever touch your watercolor paper. They are quick, sketchy little drawings of the basic shapes you are looking at. They help you to quickly move objects around your picture plane, work on value contrast and develop a basic composition for your painting.

Remember to minimize the shapes to help you work quickly. This is not a final drawing, just a way to work out the most important aspects of your painting: composition and value. If your composition and values are right, your painting will be a success.

Things to think about while developing thumbnail sketches:
• Do I want to make this painting in a horizontal or vertical format?
• Do I want all of the objects to appear in whole or do I want to cut some off at the edges?
• How can I add more interest?
• Is this painting flat or are there interesting changes in plane, line and position?
• Where is my horizon line?
• What are the basic shapes of the objects I want to add to my painting?
• How do the sizes of the shapes relate to one another?
• Are the distant objects smaller than the closer objects?
• How dark or light are the objects compared to each other?
• Where do I want the focal point or point of interest in my painting to be?
• How can I draw the viewers interest to the focal point? Use details, color, value contrast?
• Is this a subject that will keep me interested the entire time I work on it?
• What details can I leave out of this piece?
• What details are essential to the piece?
• Is this painting telling a story, expressing an idea, telling something about the artist, or simply painted for the pleasure of painting?
• Is there a dominant color in the painting?
• Are the colors leaning toward cool or warm?
• Is there a strong sense of light and dark to define the volume of the shapes?

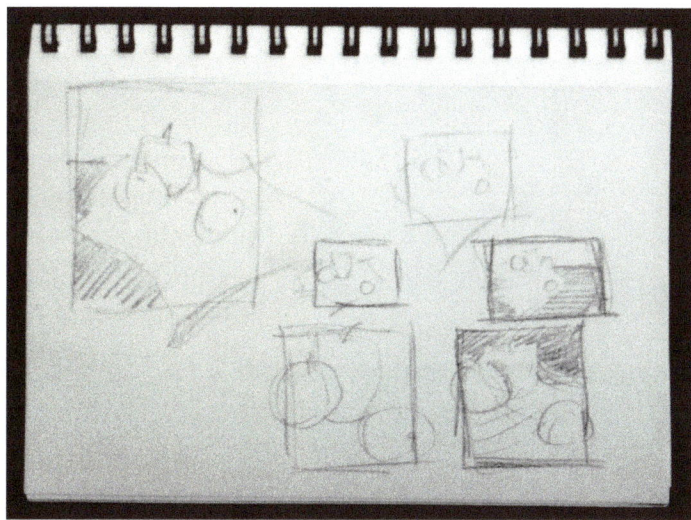

Thumbnail Sketch Process

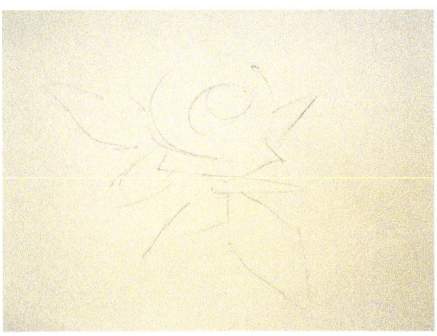

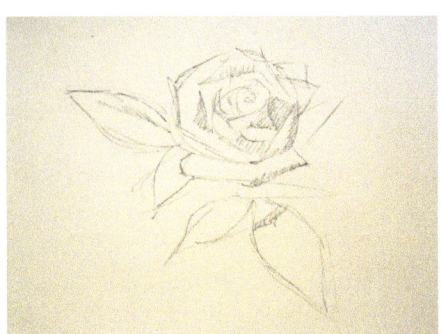

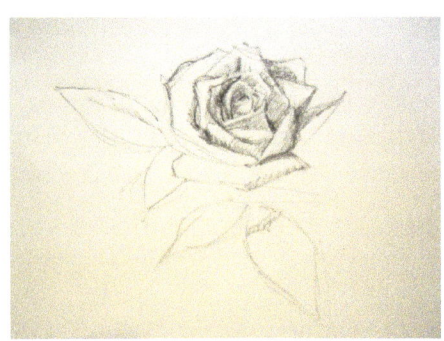

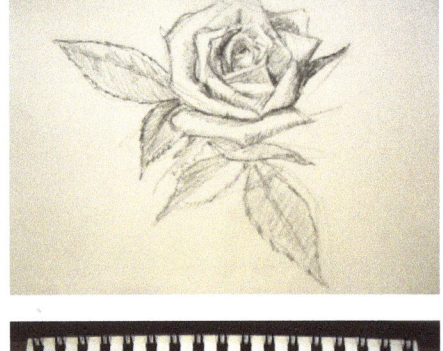

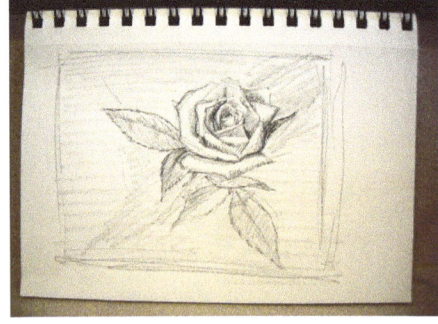

1. Look for the basic shapes in your composition.
  - Is it a triangle shape, a round shape, a rectangular shape?
  - Is it bigger on top than the bottom?
  - Is it pear-shaped?
  - Is it soft-edged, crisp, or angular?
  - Are some objects overlapping?
  - Are there spaces between objects?
  - What shapes are the "empty" areas.
  - Where does it fall in the picture plane? (Hint: draw a grid to help locate specific elements and get their relationship to one another correct.)

2. After capturing the basic outer shape of the objects, and placement on the picture plane, ask yourself the same questions from step 1 about the individual parts: shadow shapes, leaf shapes, bending petals. Also ask:
  - Do the objects reach up or swing out and down?
  - Are they close together or is there a bit of space between them?
  - Is there a crisp edge to the shadow shape or does it gently grade from dark to light?
  - Are the shapes correctly sized compared to each other?

3. Now think in values.
  - Use your value scale and think light = value 1; dark = value 6.
  - Mark the numbers 1 - 6 on your thumbnail to relate to the values.
  - If you have combined photo references for a better composition, decide the values for the added elements.
  - Pay attention to areas in shadow and in light.
  - Shade in the values according to your numbers with a pencil.

Thumbnail sketches are not final drawings. They are simply a method to work out solutions to common composition and value problems. Focus *not* on drawing but on the most basic elements of the picture.

The final drawing will be much easier after completing several thumbnail sketches.

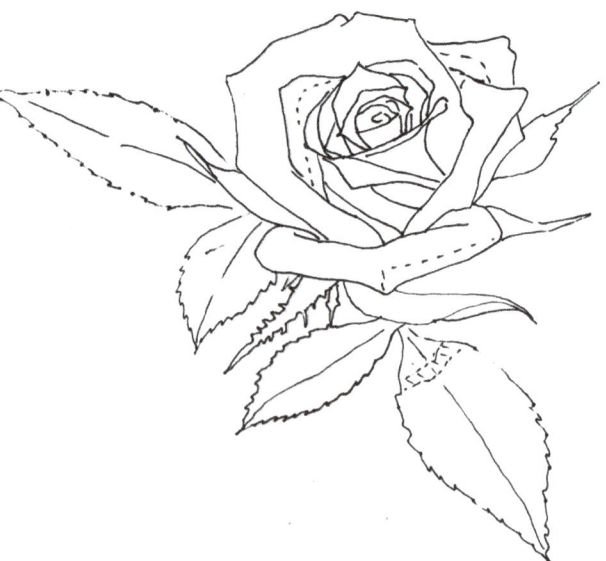

Preparing a Drawing

There are lots of ways to develop drawings for your paintings. Once you have developed a thumbnail sketch that you think fits your goals for the painting, you can then make a larger drawing, to match the size of your desired finished painting. Use this drawing to transfer to your watercolor paper.

Many of my students don't enjoy the drawing process as much as painting or simply don't have strong drawing skills, so I help them to find simpler, easier ways to develop their drawings. Many fine, professional watercolor artists use slides or computers to help them in this process. Others use a grid system, which works very well. Others simply rely on the basics in their thumbnail sketches to get the simple ideas down, then paint in a looser fashion, not worrying about the details at all.

If you have strong drawing skills, I believe that producing the drawing by hand from your references and thumbnails is the best approach. If you are anxious to paint, or don't have strong drawing skills, you can make a small drawing by tracing your photos over a light box, or hold them up to a brightly lit window. Then, when you have the basic shapes and some of the details you want to capture in your drawing you can use a photocopier to enlarge the components and place them on the proper size drawing paper for your desired painting.

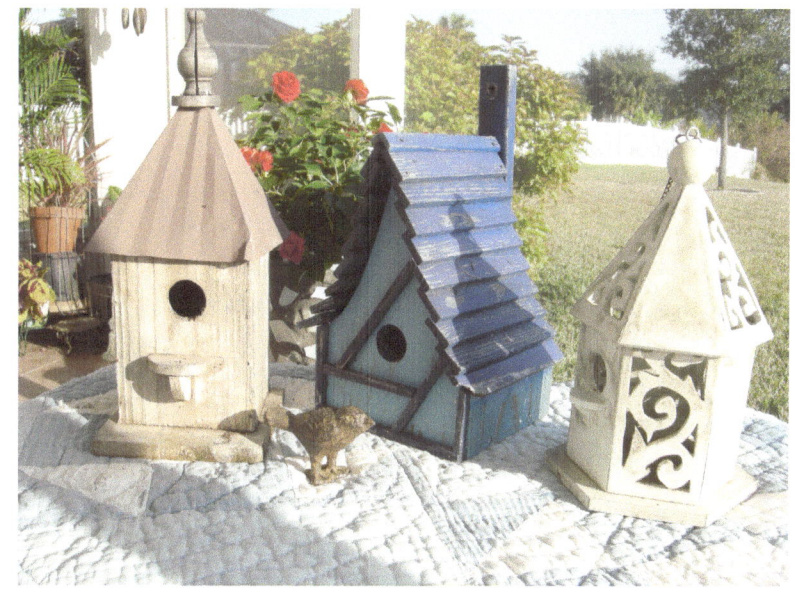

No matter how you prepare your drawing, the point that you develop it through sketching and study is crucial to a successful painting. This is the stage where you work out the road map for your painting. Take the time to sketch and get intimately familiar with the shapes and values of all the objects you want in your painting. You may even want to develop small watercolor sketches of the piece to work out color problems that may arise.

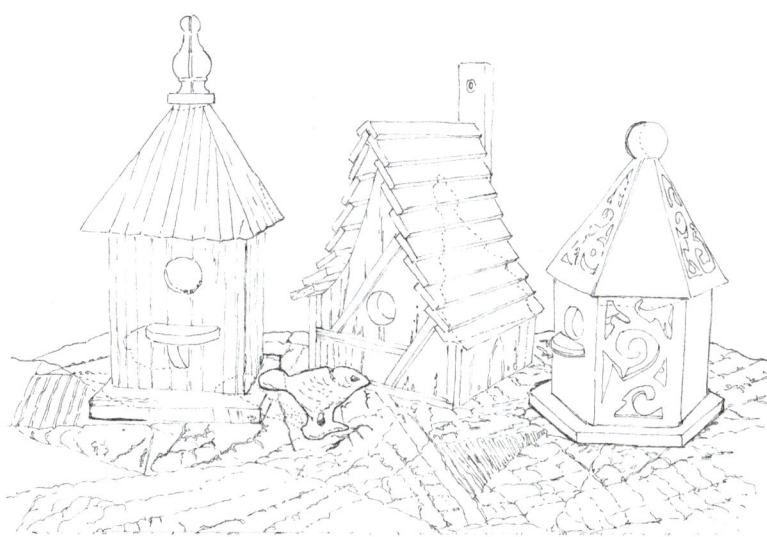

Now that you have a developed drawing, let's transfer it to your prepared watercolor paper.

Remember, the drawing should be the exact size of the desired finished painting, or the same size as your watercolor sheet.

How to Prepare Watercolor Paper

What you will need:

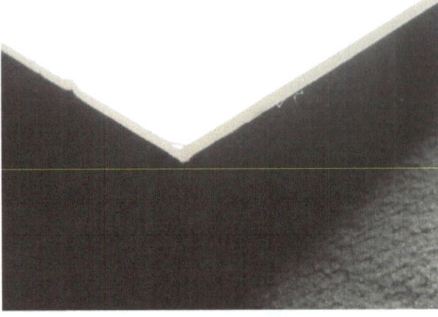

- Foam core board at least three inches bigger than your watercolor paper on all sides.
- Clear Packing Tape
- Two Inch Wide Masking Tape
- Scissors
- Watercolor Paper

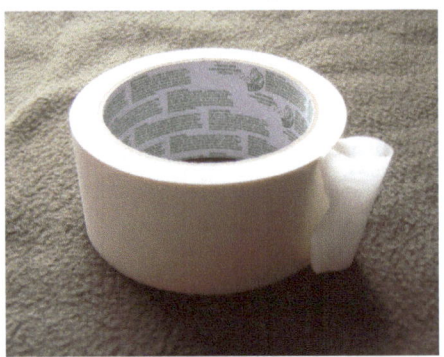

Some artists stretch wet paper onto heavy boards to keep the sheets flat while painting. I prefer this simple method of mounting dry paper onto foam core board to maintain the integrity of my paper while painting.

The process that I use protects the areas of the foam core board where you will eventually tape your watercolor paper. The clear packing tape prevents the masking tape from tearing the foam core and it slightly waterproofs the edges to protect it when applying juicy washes onto your painting. This board, if properly prepared, will be useful for many paintings in the future. It is a lightweight alternative to traditional watercolor paper stretching.

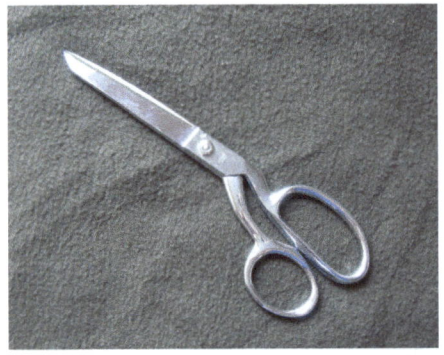

1. Cut foam core so that it measures about two inches larger than your watercolor paper on all sides.

2. Tape the outer edges of the foam core with clear packing tape. Cover the edges with at least two rows of tape on all sides, front and back. This board may be used over and over again as a support to your watercolor paper.

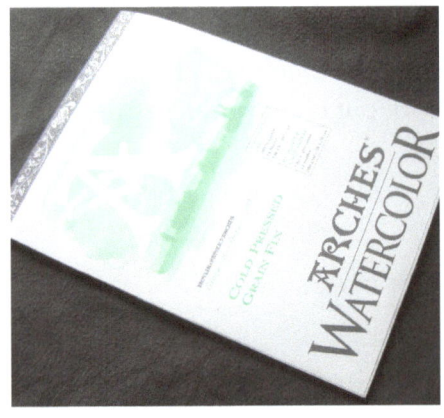

3. Tape watercolor paper to prepared foam core board with masking tape. Be sure that at least 1/2 inch of your watercolor paper is covered with the tape to secure it to the board. Remember, your paper will get wet while painting. This will cause it to buckle, warp and stretch. The secure application of tape will hold it firmly to the foam core during the painting process.

4) Now you are ready to transfer a drawing to your paper.

Your framer will appreciate the fact that your artwork was stretched to stay more flat. Framing a warmed and bowed watercolor is very difficult.

Transfer the Drawing to Watercolor Paper

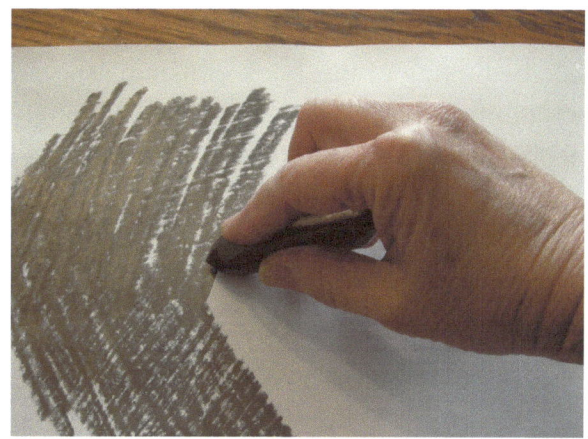

What you will need:
• Watercolor paper
• Completed drawing and thumbnail sketches
• Photo references
• Chunky graphite stick
• Pencil for tracing
• Prepared foam core stabilizer board
• Two inch wide masking tape

1. Scrub the chunky graphite stick on the back of your completed drawing. Use a little elbow grease to get good coverage over the entire image area.

2. Use a tissue to gently smooth over the graphite to release loose crumbs and to fill in the spaces where the graphite didn't completely cover the paper. Use a light touch.

3. Wash your hands! This will keep your watercolor paper clean.

4. Use a strip of masking tape and secure the drawing on one edge to your watercolor paper, like a hinge. This will allow you to lift the drawing occasionally to check your progress, without losing your alignment.

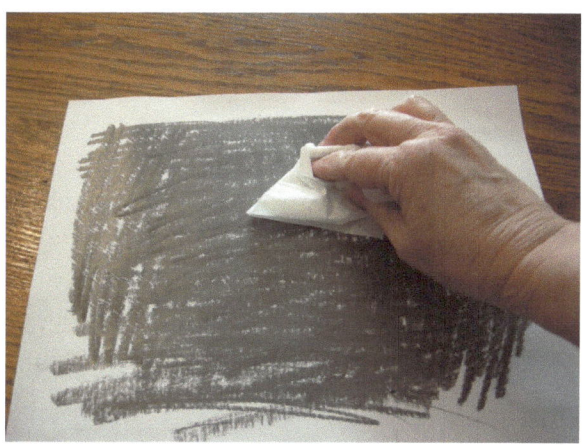

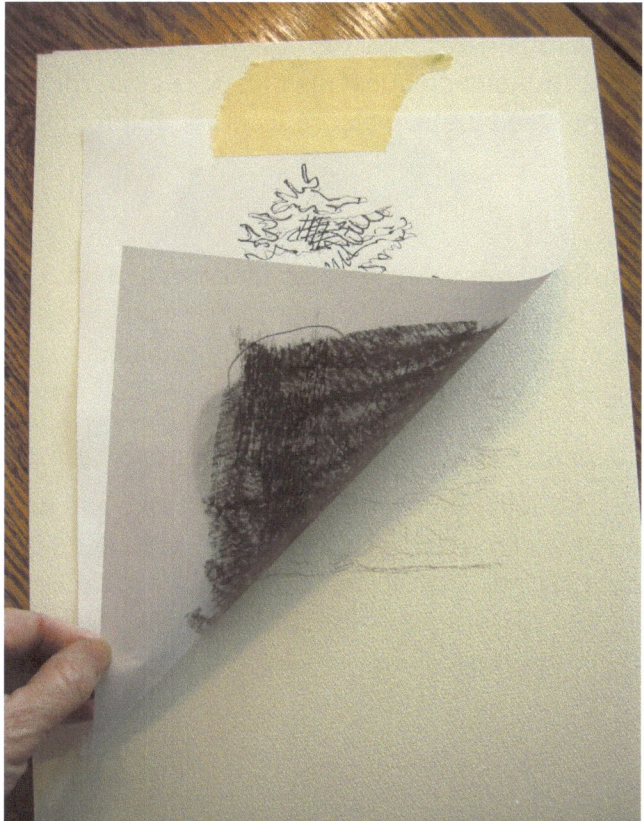

5. Trace your image using a pencil or an ink pen. Be gentle so that you do not dent the watercolor paper. You only need to press enough to deposit the graphite image lightly onto the paper.

6. Carefully lift off the drawing paper and fold it in half so that the graphite is on the inside.

7. Now you can use a pencil to correct any markings you may want to fix. Using a white vinyl eraser you may also gently erase places where you don't want the graphite.

8. Place your watercolor paper on the prepared foam core board. Secure it with the masking tape. Be sure to cover at least 1/2" of the paper edges with the tape to keep it from buckling when wet.

9. Now you are ready to paint!!!

An alternative method is to use graphite transfer paper purchased from an art supply store.

Let's Paint!

Using either the transfer technique shown at the beginning of this book or using a sheet of graphite transfer paper (do not use carbon paper!), transfer the drawing onto a small sheet of Arches watercolor paper, 140 lb. is fine. Eight by eight inches is a good size since this is a very small painting.

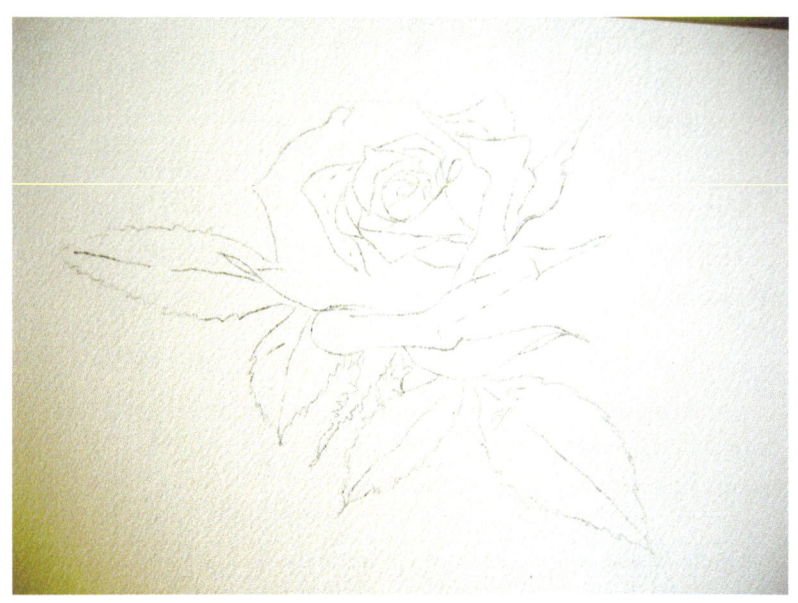

I used what I call the Push-Pull Stroke and the Softened Edge Stroke for most of this painting. If you haven't viewed my YouTube links on brushwork, you can find them on the Lessons page tab on my website. Preview the brush work techniques, then give it a try on the flower.

To review the brush strokes I will just take a moment to review.

The Push-Pull Stroke: Make a puddle of color on your palette. You will use a number 8 or 10 round brush. Load the brush with color and lightly touch it to a paper towel in order to avoid drips on the watercolor paper. Hold the brush nearly straight up and down vertically. Lightly touch the brush to the paper and pull it

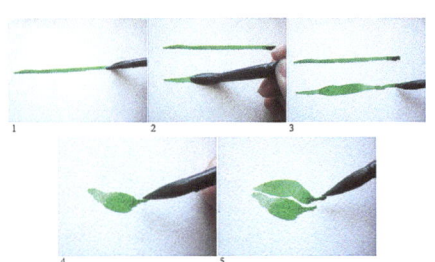

along varying the pressure from light to heavy to create a varied, thick-thin line. Try this stroke again and instead of just pulling the brush in one direction, create a zig-zag, and then completely change the direction of the stroke as you continue to pull and vary the pressure. This creates a beautiful multi-directional stroke that varies in width. It is great for organic line work, details for wood grain, water reflections, and for the edges of flowers and leaves.

The Softened Edge Stroke: This stroke is similar to the Push-Pull Stroke, but with an additional effect. Use a wet pigment, and load a round brush with color, touch gently to a paper towel to remove any excess pigment that might drip. Hold the brush in a vertical position. Gently pull the loaded brush a short distance on the paper. Quickly rinse the brush and touch it again to the paper towel to remove any drips. Push the water-loaded brush from the white of the paper into the line of pigment and along the edge of the stroke. This will push clear water into the edge of the stroke to "soften" the edge. Be careful not to pull the pigment from the

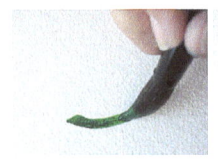 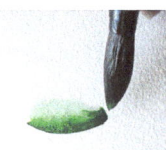

stroke to the white of the paper. This will dilute the initial stroke and just pull pigment out onto the white paper. The goal is to soften the edge of the stroke without diluting it and we want to avoid a dirty line of faded pigment when the stroke dries. Always pull water into the stroke from the white paper and not the other direction.

I used Quinacridone Magenta, New Gamboge and Permanent Alizarine Crimson for the starting pigments. I began with the petals. Using both the Pull-Push Stroke and the Softened Edge Stroke, I worked around the petals, avoiding edges that touched one another until they were dry. Looking for shadow areas, I applied the Alizarin Crimson, and added Quinacridone Magenta and New Gamboge depending upon the color and light called for. Some areas of the petals have a white/blue spot where the light is striking them directly. These areas are softened with water only, no pigment is needed here as the white of the paper becomes the highlight. Moisture is needed though, to keep the edges soft.

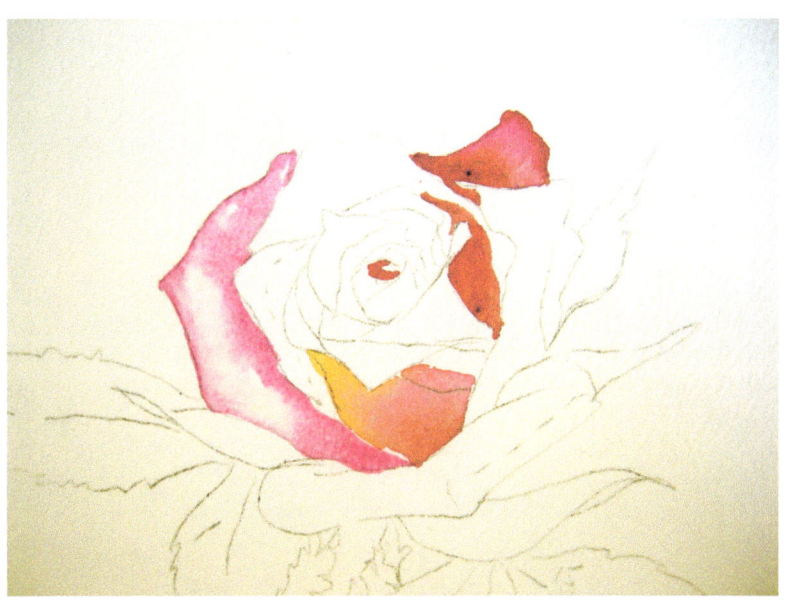

You can see on the bottom rose petal here where I painted the Softened Edge Stroke. I applied very wet, fairly concentrated pigment, then rinsed my brush, dabbed it lightly on my blotter (paper toweling) and brushed clear water alongside and into the wet pigment that was just applied. Pushing the water from the white of the paper into the previous stroke creates a soft edged transition from light to dark. This stroke pushes the pigment particles to the darker side of the stroke and keeps the soft edge very smooth. It takes a little practice to master this one, but it is a very useful brush stroke.

I worked around the rose petals with tiny washes of three pigments, a yellow, a pink, and a cool red for the shadows.

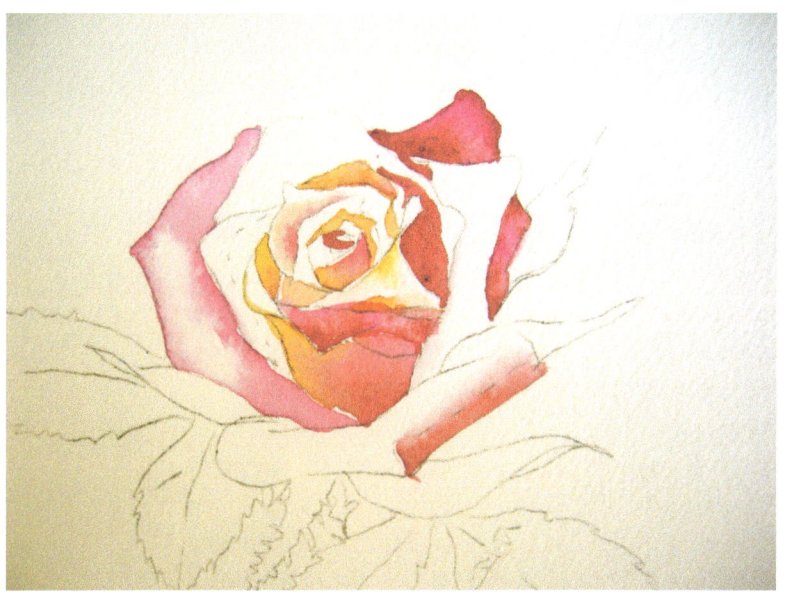

I had to work around and around, so that one petal may dry before I paint the one right next to it. If the wet edges touch they will run together. Notice that there are cool (dark red, plum) and warm areas (light pink and golden). This is because when the light hits the different edges of the petals it bounces around and casts different hues – the lighter side, facing the light source, will have warmer colors including in the shadows, and the side that faces away from the light source will contain much cooler colors, not just darker colors. Understanding this helps to build a believable painting.

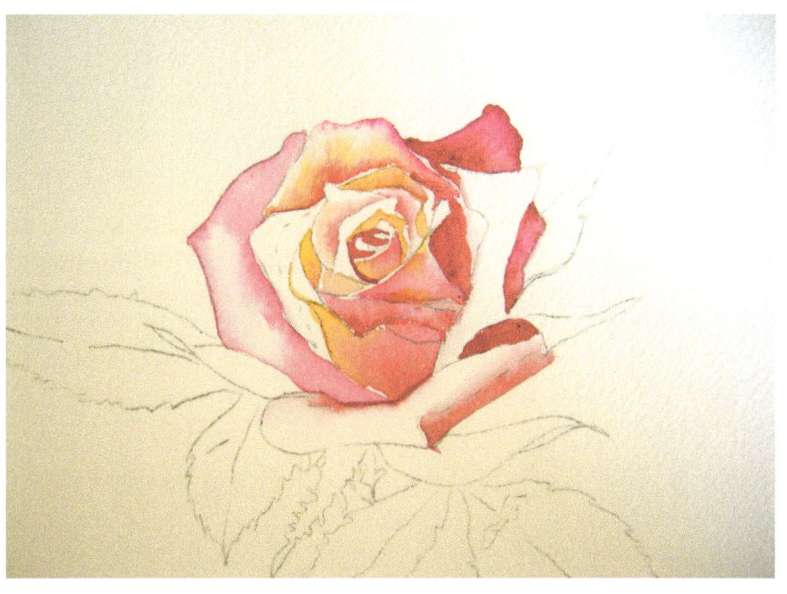

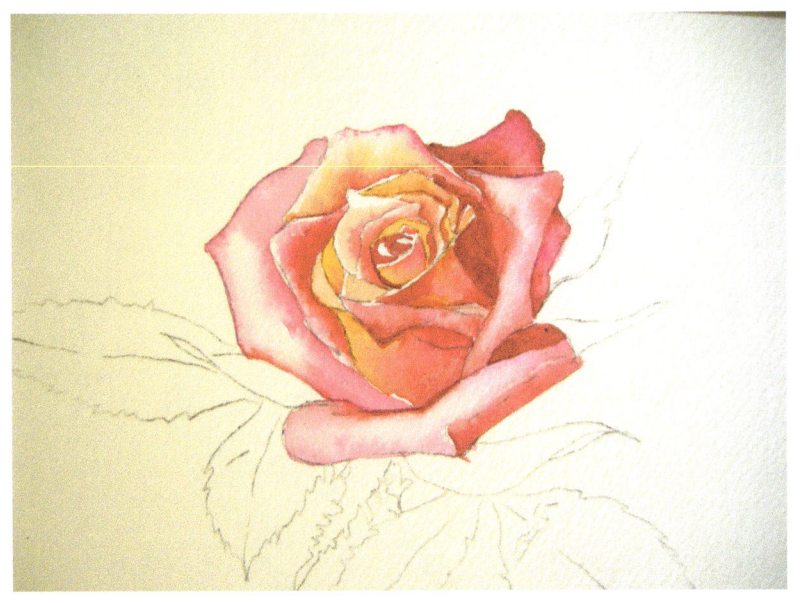

The rose is nearly completed at this point. Now that most of the petals are completed, I can see how the colors, values (lights and darks), and shapes work to create the illusion of a three-dimensional flower. Notice that I left tiny white areas at the tops of some of the petals. I want to leave these so that the edges between petals are shiny, clear and vivid. These little white areas help the painting to sparkle, and also help to set off the darker shadows just under the edges of the petal's white edge.

In nature, leaves on the same plant will bounce around in the light and have a multitude of colors. Some will look blue, some will look green, others will look yellow or brown. In order for the painting to represent nature, a variety of colors should be worked into the leaves. For the yellow-green areas I used a very watery mixture of New Gamboge and Permanent Sap Green. I applied it softly and thoughtfully, not completely filling in the outline, but carefully looking at the photo reference to guide me where to place the color and whether or not to create soft or crisp edges. The applications of paint here are really an under-painting for future glazes of color that will be gently layered over the tops of these pigments.

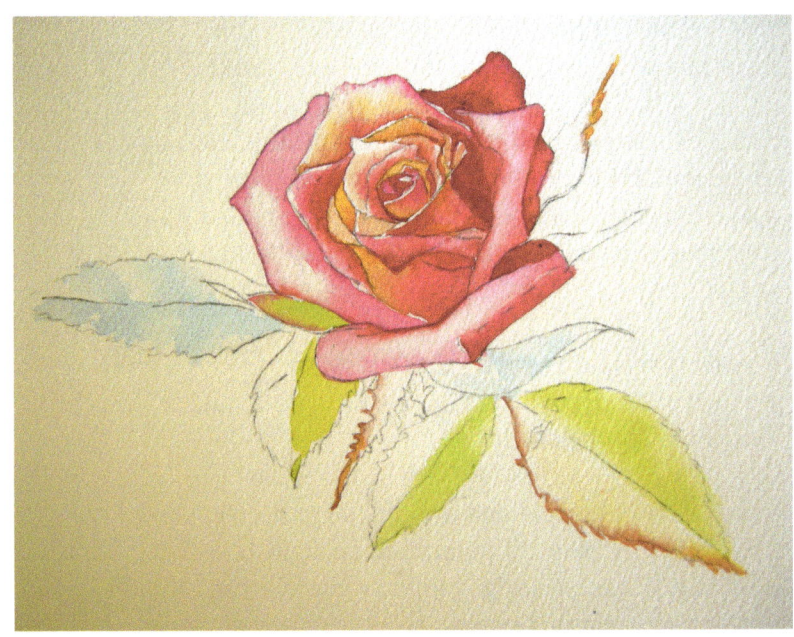

The blue is a very wet, wet, wet application of Pthalo blue. Be careful with this color – it is extremely intense. There should only be a hint of color and lots of water. Notice that some of the edges are softened with water.

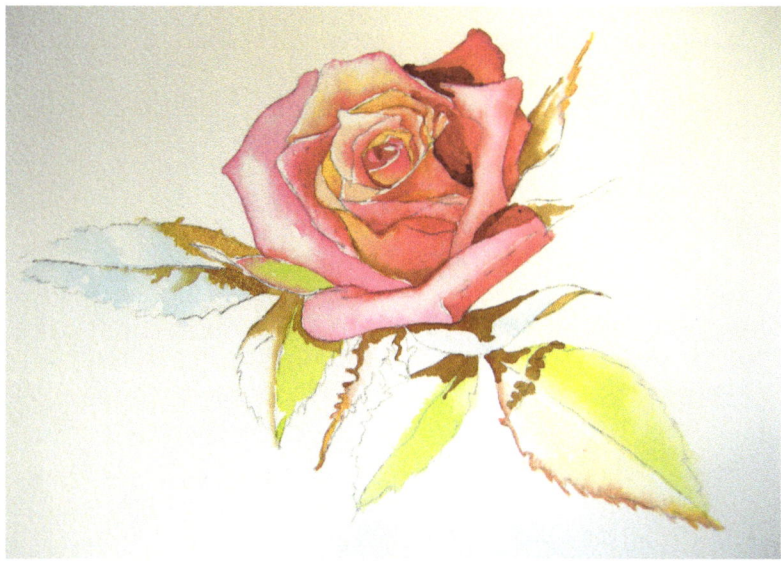

I used Burnt Sienna to create the delicate red-brown edges of some of the leaves. Again, to keep it looking natural I did not apply this to every edge, only some. I also used Burnt Sienna to create an under-painting for the darker, cast shadows on the leaves.

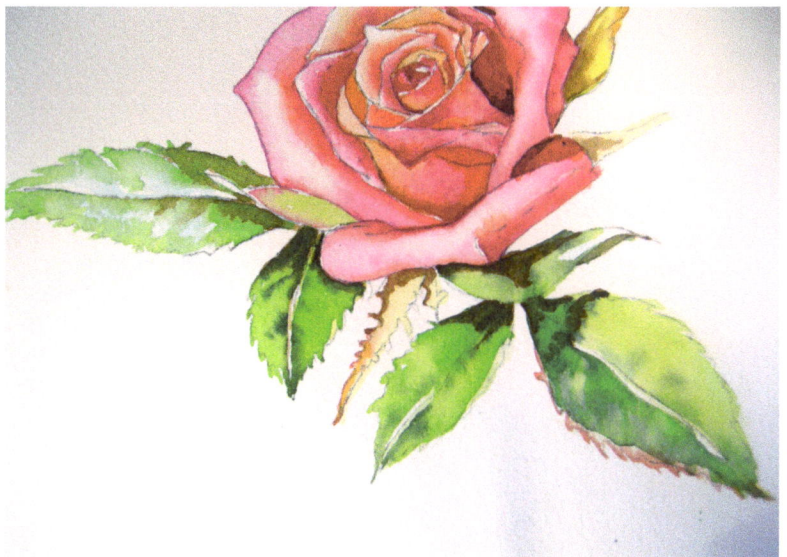

Once all of the previous layers are dried completely, I can add glazes of green and yellow. I used several combinations of wet applications with New Gamboge, Permanent Sap Green and Hookers Green. Notice how the "brown" shadows become dark green when the green pigments are glazed on. Be careful not to stroke your brush over these areas too much, be gentle, or the previous layers will lift and create "mud".
I applied these greens with very wet, gentle strokes. Then, dipping my brush into darker colors, I touched the darker colors into the wet areas to create very soft shadows. It is important to let the pigment do what it wants to do here. Don't try to control it too much.

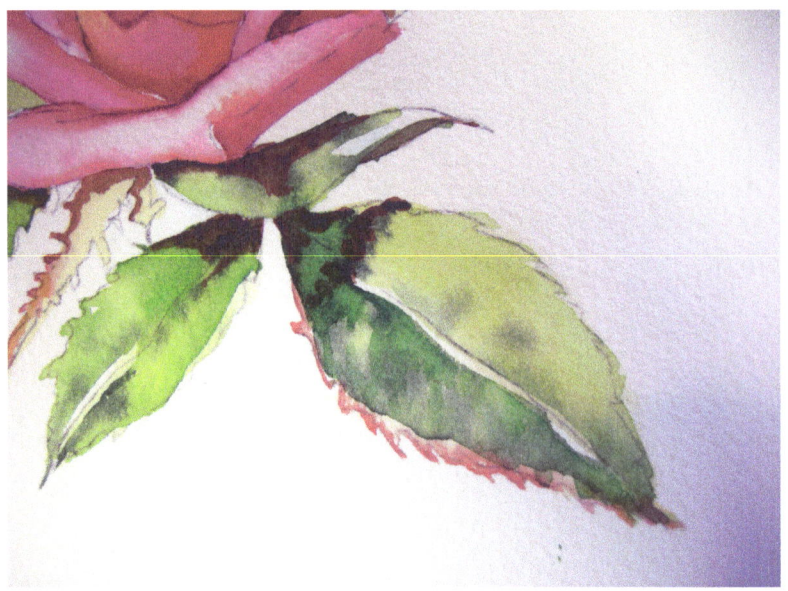

Here is a detail shot of the bottom leaf. I think of butterfly kisses when I'm painting these areas. Just "tickle" the paper with your brush, using almost no pressure at all. Be thoughtful where the tip of your brush touches the wet areas with darker color, and let it blend on its own. You can tip the paper and allow gravity to move the pigment if you want it to move more. Don't strive for "perfection", but strive for "sparkle".

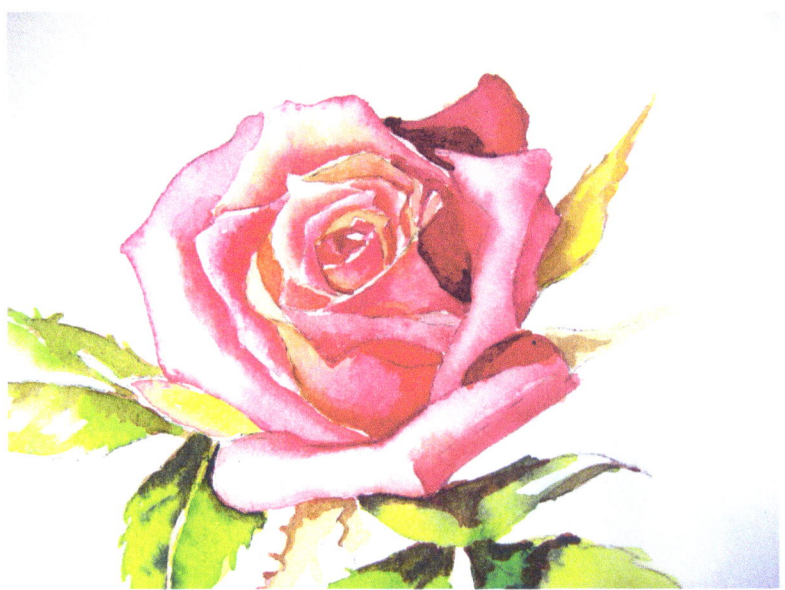

Okay, almost done with the rose!

As I looked at the overall painting, I wanted to add some more "punch" to the shadows of the rose petals. The more value ranges (dark to light), the more depth I can create to make it look truly three-dimensional.

I used some Perylene Maroon to add a touch of dark red to the deepest shadows of my flower. Now the light areas really "pop"!

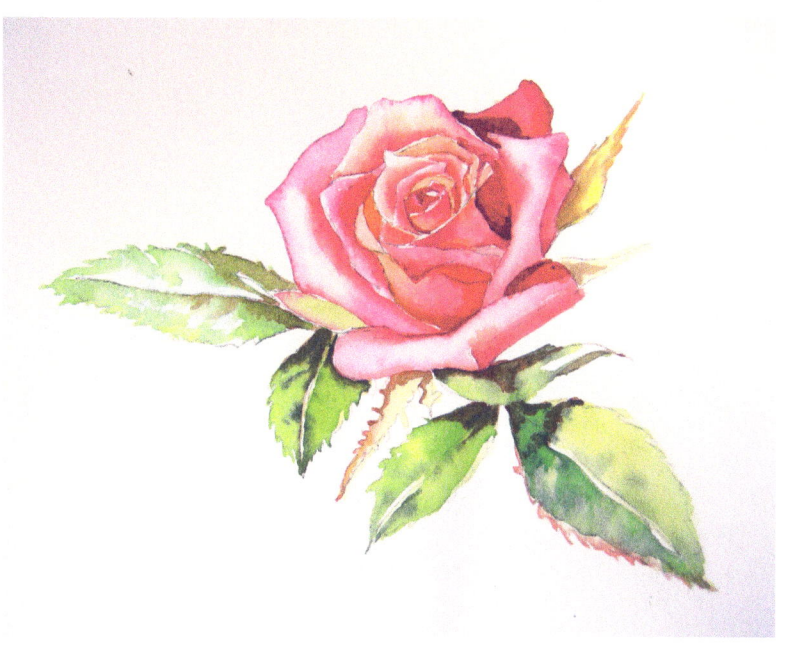

I have a little philosophy that once I sign a painting I cannot add anything more to it. It works well to keep me from over-working a painting!

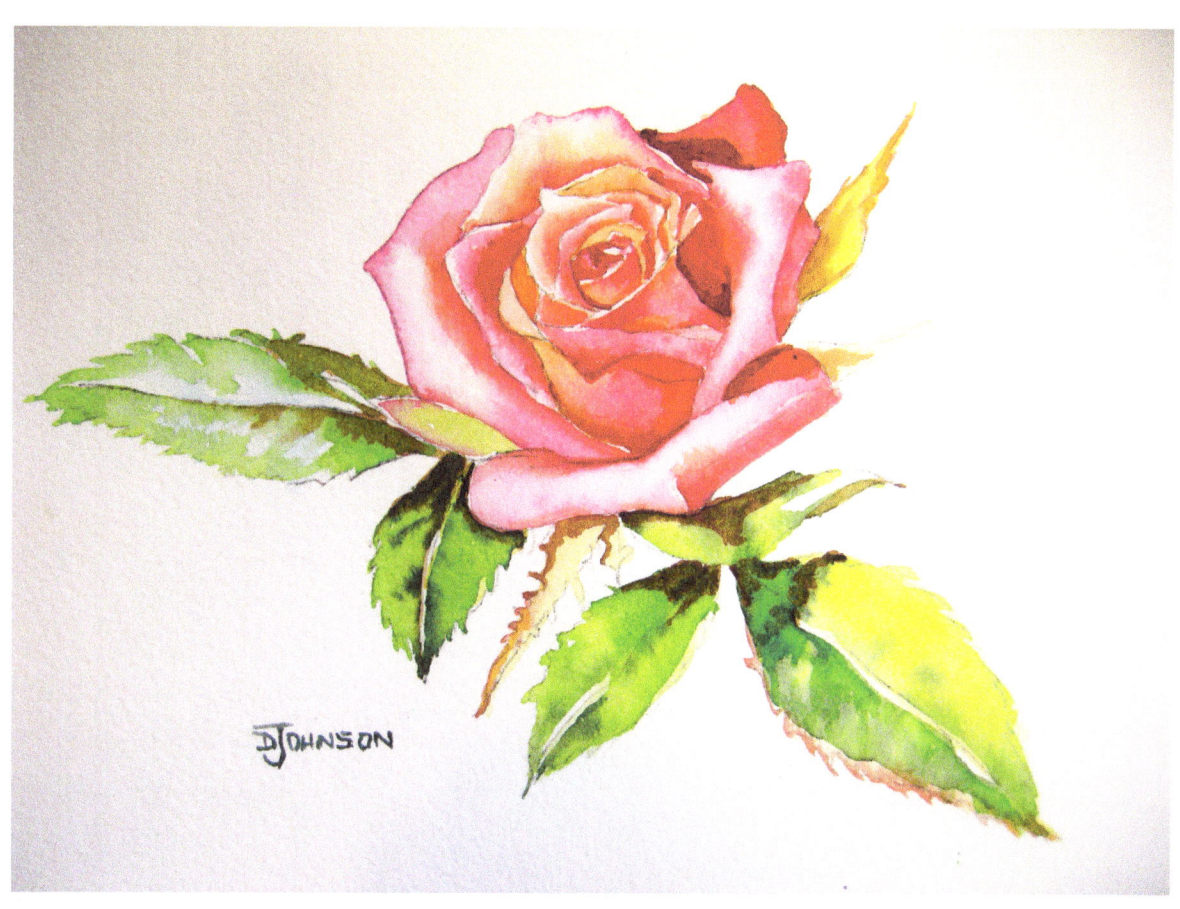

So, signed and complete – the finished Pink Rose!

Reference Photos

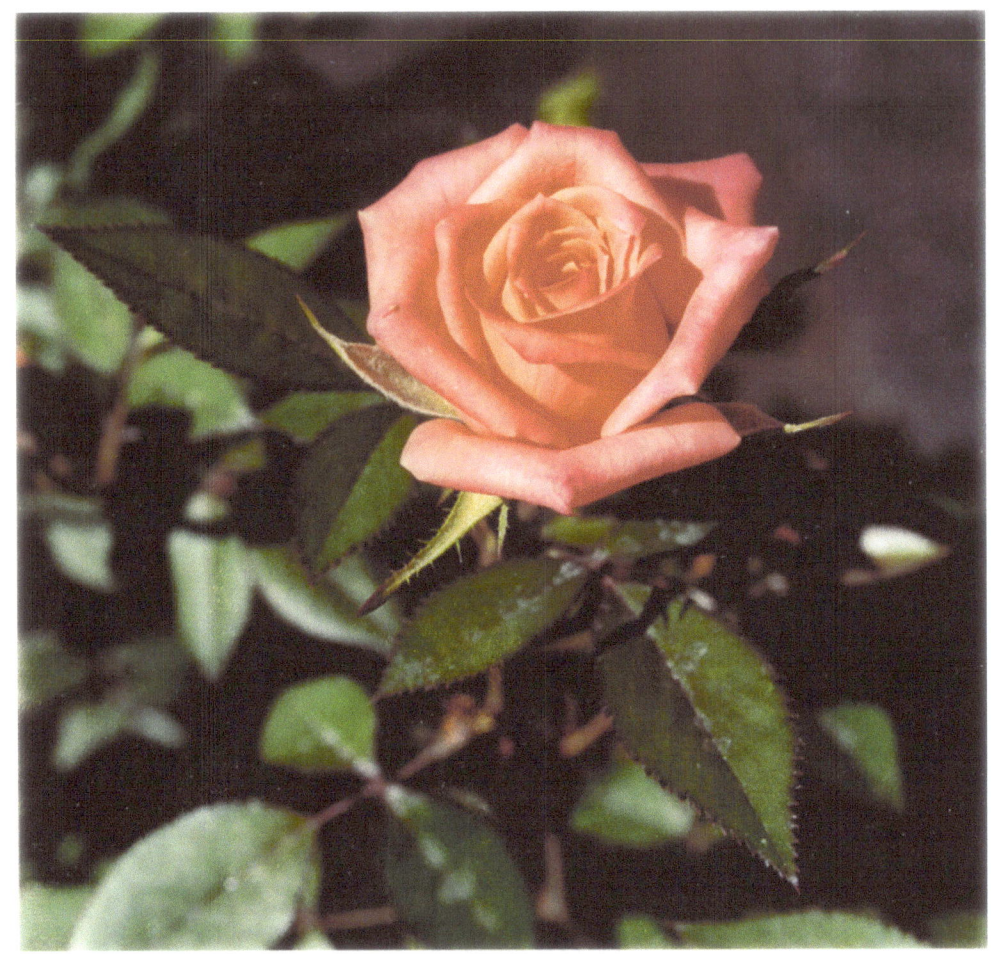

Removing the color from the reference photo helps me to see the values, the lights and darks, in the photo which give the two dimensional surface of the photo an illusion of space and shape.

The black and white photo helps me to see the shapes of the dark and light colors which help to define the shape and dimension of the objects.

Look at the value chart below and try to see where those values are represented in the grayscale photo reference.

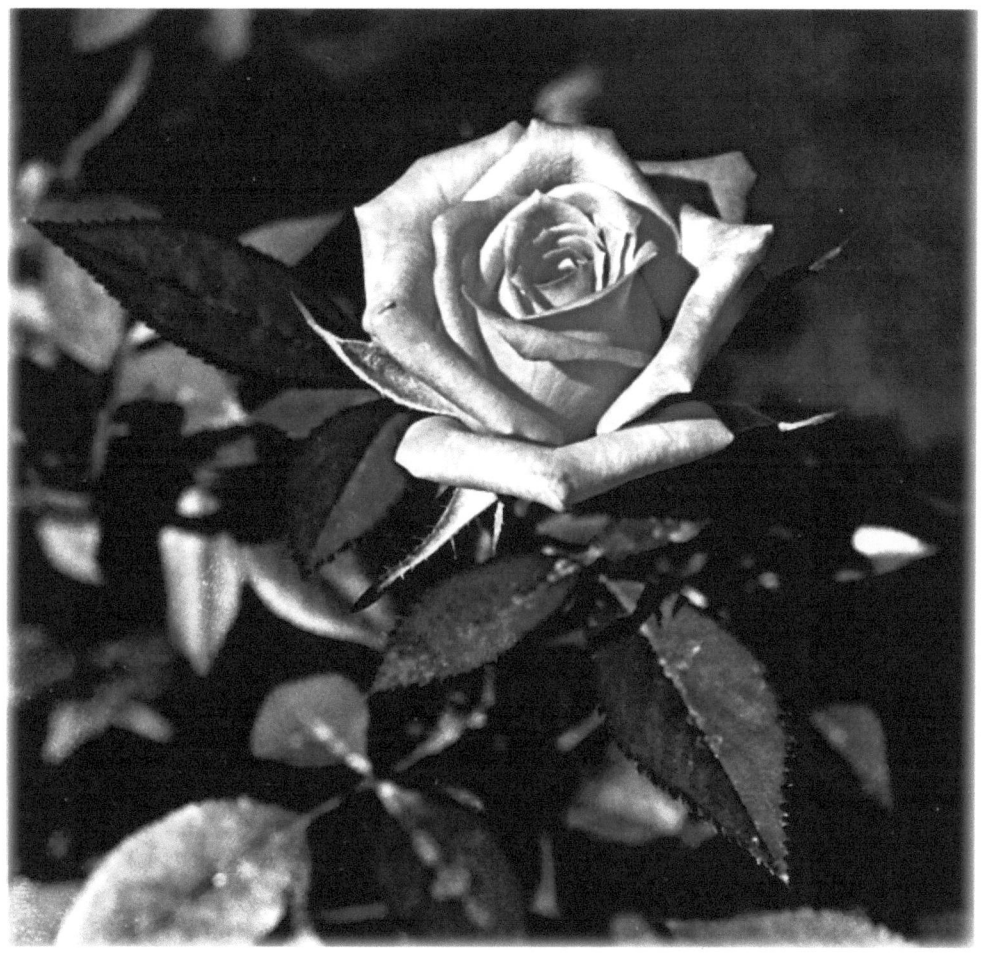

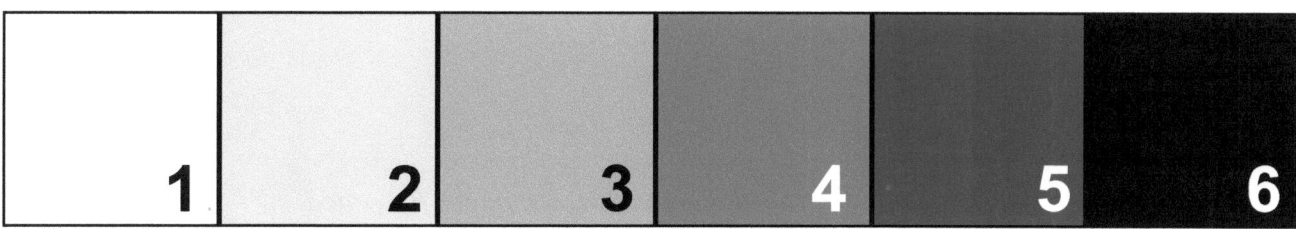

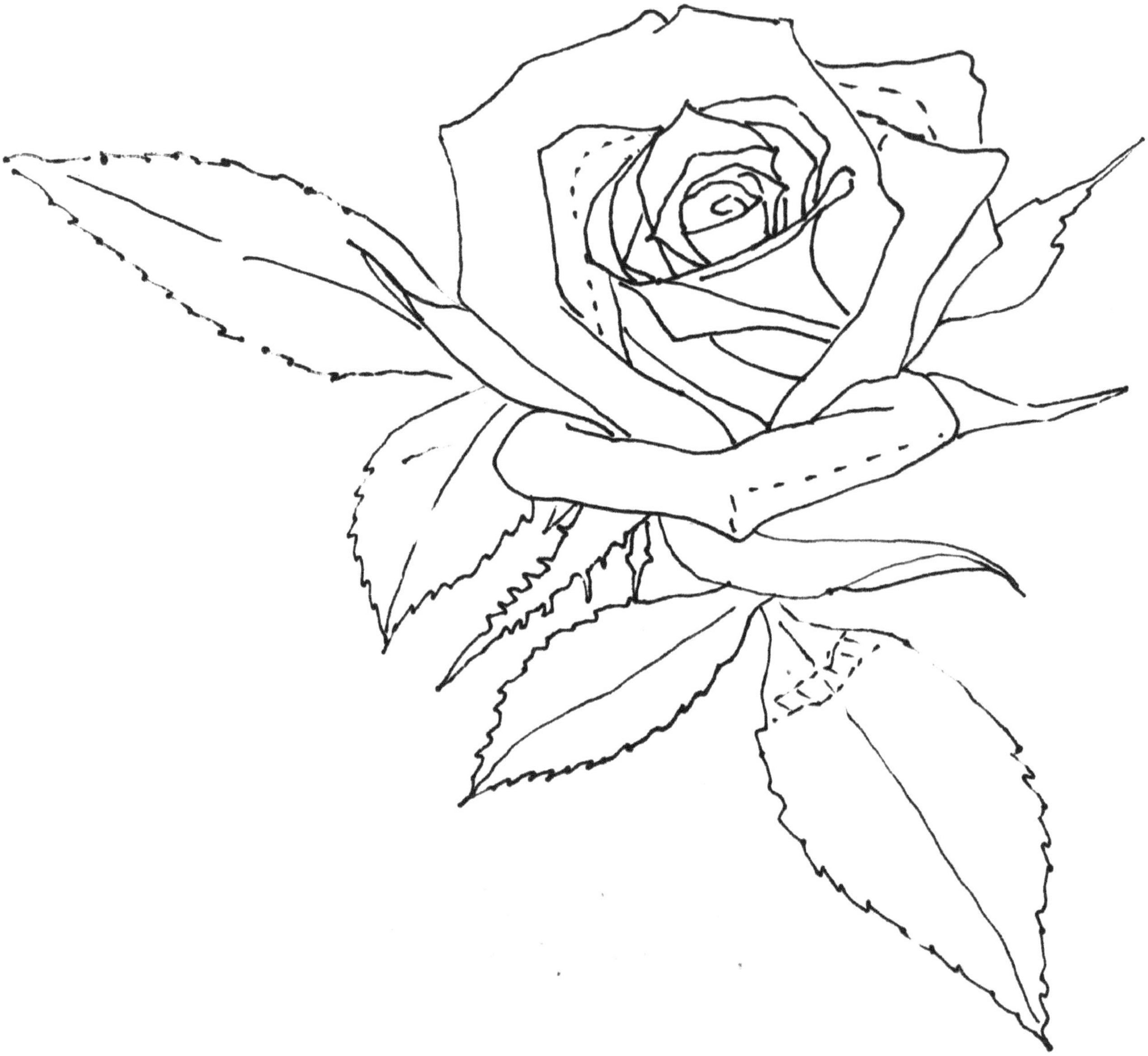

This drawing can be traced onto watercolor paper for practice.
This page may be copied or enlarged for your personal use only.

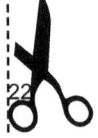

Suggested Watercolor Supplies

- 11" x 14" pad of Arches 140 lb. watercolor paper, or larger
- 1" Flat brush, natural hair, or natural hair/synthetic blend
- No. 10 round brush, natural hair or natural hair/synthetic blend
- No. 6 round brush, natural hair or natural hair/synthetic blend
- Palette with large mixing wells and 1" or wider paint wells
  My favorite palette is CheapJoes Piggy Back.
- Windsor Newton (Professional Grade/not student grade) Pigments: Aureolin Yellow, New Gamboge, Winsor Red, Permanent Alizarin Crimson, Burnt Sienna, Raw Umber, Hookers Green, Cerulean Blue, French Ultramarine Blue, Indigo. Any other colors you may like to use. Other good brands are: Maimeriblu, Holbein, and Daler-Rowney. Look for transparent colors.
- White Vinyl Eraser
- Sketchbook, any kind
- Large water container (1 lb. deli tub works great)
- Paper Towel
- No. 2 Pencil
- 2" Wide Masking Tape (Not blue painter's tape)
- Masking Fluid
- Masking Fluid Brush
- Two small containers for masking and soap.

Have fun experimenting with colors, brushes, and techniques. Every artist has their favorite tools and methods which is what makes them unique.

Great Online Art Supply Resources:
www.cheapjoes.com
jerrysartarama.com
www.dickblick.com
www.aswexpress.com
www.utrechtart.com
www.artsuppliesonline.com
Be sure to check with your local art supply store first.

Debbie Waldorf Johnson has more lessons on her website:
http://debbiejohnsonartist.wordpress.com/Lessons
You will find step-by-step lessons in blog format as well as links to videos of how to correctly develop watercolor washes.

www.ingramcontent.com/pod-product-compliance
Lightning Source LLC
Chambersburg PA
CBHW050435180526
45159CB00006B/2548